How to Retire Happy & Financially Secure!

26 Low Stress & Easy Ways to Retire Happy and Financially Secure

By

Pete & Kimberly Peters

All rights Reserved 2014 – 26Ways.com

Also Available from 26Ways.com:

26 Ways to Get More Fun from RC Aircraft

26 Ways to Save Money on Your Utility Bills

26 Ways to Manage Your Type 2 Diabetes & Control Your Blood sugar

26 Ways to Become A Better Manager

26 Ways to Grow Your On-Line Business

26 Ways to Be the Best Wife Ever!

For all other Publications, and for more information on our books and manuals, please visit our website at:

http://www.26ways.com

Contents

Introduction	5
Start Early	10
Live Within Your Means	13
Be Realistic	17
Pay Yourself Not Uncle Sam!	20
Invest Wisely & Responsibly	23
Lower Rates Means More Savings!	28
The 100 Plan	32
Medical Costs	35
Your Credit Rating	37
Retirement is a Work in Progress	41
1. Play the Match Game!	45
2. Even a Little Means a Lot	47
3. Pay Yourself First	49
4. Payroll Deduction	50
5. Pre-Tax Bliss	52
6. Post Tax Blast	54
7. Split that Raise	56
8. Tax Refund Boost	58
9. Bonus Time Bonanza!	60
10. Mortgage Muscle	62
11. Minimize Fees	66
12. Reduce High Cost Interest	68
13. Create a Budget NOW!	72
14. Give the Gift of Retirement!	76
15. Know Your Social Security	78
16. Bank a Part Time Income	80
17. Start a Small Home Based Business	82
18. Health & Long Term Care Insurance	86
19. Retirement First, Kids Second	90
20. Save When Downsizing	94
21. Catch up Savings	97
22. Asset Protection & Estate Planning	98
23. Your Home	102
24. No Premature Withdrawals!	105
25. Plan Last Minute Major Purchases	109
26. Postponing Retirement	115

27. Supplementing Retirement	**120**
28. After Retirement	**122**
Conclusion	**124**

Disclaimer

The information contained in this book is designed and provided for informational puposes only. It is not designed or intended for use on any specific situation or application. Since everyone is different and everyone's situation is different, some or all of the information presented in this book may or may not be appropriate or applicable for any particular individual. The writers, publishers and sellers of this book assume no responsibility for the use or application of all or any part of this publication. The reader assumes total responsibility for determining which information, if any, is appropriate for their given situation. In all matters that contain a financail component, it is strongly suggested that one consult or retain a knowledgeable and reputable financial advisor to provide appropriate guidance and specific information.

Introduction

Retirement can be a wonderful part of life as long as you prepare for it. So many people have dreams of spending their retirement sitting on the beach in Hawaii and then when they actually retire they realize they have to work part time at the local Walmart to make ends meet!

For most of us, the reality will be somewhere between those two extremes. Which lifestyle we will eventually wind up with will depend on what we do now that will help prepare us for what happens later. The key is to prepare ourselves for all parts of our lives now so the burden is equally spread around with much less impact on our overall quality of life.

This book is not written by stock traders or financial consultants who just want you to sock away as much as you can so they can make more commissions and earn larger salaries. On the contrary, it is written by people just like you who just want to retire comfortably with few worries when it comes to money.

You will not see anything for sale in this book and we offer no financial products or services.

This book is strictly for your benefit and we are going to tell you just how it is when it comes to retirement. It is up to you to decide if what we are talking about makes sense or not. You will probably find some things in this book that really make you sit up and take notice because they hit home for you.

Other things might not pertain to you or your situation and that is fine as well. There is no "one size fits all" approach to retirement. Your financial plan will probably be different than your brothers or sisters and it will definitely be different from your mom and dad's retirement plan.

That is because the word today has changed so much over the last few decades. It used to be just a dream of retiring a millionaire but today that is usually not enough for most people to retire on! This is because life has changed, our expenses have changed and because there are a lot more things to spend money on today than our parents had.

Lifespans have increased as well. That means that not only will you have a greater chance of living longer, your retirement nest egg will have to last you longer!

So you will have to save more money or invest it at higher yields so that you will have enough money to live on until your time comes.

The great thing is that with just a little planning and some common sense, you can retire comfortably with very little effect on your lifestyle or standard of living.

In other words, you will have to sacrifice but nowhere near as much as you might have thought. But you need to get started right now. Not tomorrow or next year but right now.

This book is a great way to get started or to increase your ability to save for your retirement. But before we get started there are a few things about this book that we would like you to know.

First of all, feel free to jump around if you see something that really interests you or that you think will benefit you right now. We have written this book so that you can start at any point, skip around from topic to topic, and still understand everything that is written. In order to do this, however, you might notice a few things that are repeated more than once. This is not a mistake but rather done on purpose because some things pertain to more than one topic or concept. The good thing is that these items are usually also among the most important or critical information and reading them a few times will help you retain the information for longer periods of time.

Second, although you can skip around, we strongly suggest that you read the first section of this book first. This section covers attitudes and overall concepts pertaining to retirement and what you need to understand so you can adequately prepare yourself.

This information is important and will be the basis for everything moving forward.

So please read the first section all the way through first to get the foundation for what will follow.

Third, most goals in life are achieved through constant effort and by taking small steps. Very few noteworthy goals are accomplished by one massive action or grand gesture. So don't think that you have to make huge changes or save massive amounts of money from day one. If you try and do too much all at once, the sacrifice will be too great and you will not be able to sustain your efforts. It is far better to start off small, take one thing at a time and find a plan that you can stick with and that will help you achieve your goal.

OK! Let's get started!

Part One:

Retirement Saving Philosophy

Start Early

If I had to give the single most important piece of advice to anyone thinking about saving towards retirement, it would be to start as early as possible. This will not only enable you to save more money over a longer period of time, it will allow you money to work longer and harder for you at the same time.

The problem is that when people are in their early twenties, they usually don't think about retirement. They don't think about how long they are going to live or how they are going to live their lives. They don't think about medical issues, cost of living and how they are going to live and function in the years to come.

That is because at that age they feel invincible. They feel like they are going to live forever and live happily ever after. They do not do this out of stupidity or irresponsibility, they do it because they do not have the life experience to understand why these things are so important.

Because of this, they start planning for the future during later stages of life and years of savings opportunities are lost forever.

That means to accomplish the same end goal you have to save more every month which usually entails more sacrifice and will power.

Starting early enable our savings to grow at a faster rate by using the concept of compound interest. Compound interest means that for every year you have money invested, it earns you more money. For example, if you invest $1,000 at 5% interest, at the end of one year you would have $1,050. But the next you if the interest rate was still 5% you would get the interest on $1,050 instead of the original $1,000 which means you would then get $52.50 interest that year instead of the previous year's $50.

This might not sound like a lot but every year the interest gets more and more and the principal amount gets more as you add to it. Think about the difference when you have $300,000 or $500,000 earning interest for you!

Starting early also means that to reach the same goals you would have to save less per year. So the effect on your lifestyle and standard of living would be much less. If you wait until you are 40 or 50 to start saving you might find that you have to save so much each year that it would be impossible for you to reach your goals! Even if you could, your lifestyle would take a huge hit!

But regardless of this, some of you might already have escaped your 20 and even your 30's already. That does not mean that it is too late to make a meaningful difference if you start now. Whether you are 19 or 49 years of age, you will have an easier time saving if you start today. If you are 19 don't wait until you are 20. If you are 39 don't wait until you are 40. Start today, not tomorrow.

And also do not think that because you cannot save thousands of dollars that it isn't worthwhile to save at all and that it is OK to wait until you are earning more money of have fewer expenses. Because there will always be something to spend money on and there will always be excuses. Even if you save just $100 a year in your 20's you would have over $1,000 plus interest when you hit 30. If you had not saved anything, you would have nothing. So even $1,000 is better than nothing. Plus, it will have 30-40 years of compound interest to turn that $1,000 into 5 or possibly $10,000!

Everything in this book will work better for you when you start early. But regardless of your age when you start everything will still help you reach your final goals. But don't wait another day, month or year to get started. Start now no matter whether you can save $100 or $10,000. Every little bit helps.

If you have children now, start talking to them about the need to save now. Get it into their heads at an early age. If you don't have children yet, think about this when you do. Setting a good example for them now and giving them the knowledge they need to succeed is one of the greatest gifts you can possible give them.

Live Within Your Means

Though many people, even most people, don't realize it, what we do today can have a profound effect on how we live tomorrow and how much money we have in our retirement accounts when it comes time to retire. Because of this, it makes sense to be aware of how we live today so it doesn't sabotage our plans for retirement.

Think about your retirement nest egg as a combination of what you have saved minus whatever your debts are when you retire. If you saved $2,000,000 by the time you retire you might think you had done a great job and you would be right. But if you also had debts of $2,000,000 then you really have nothing at all when it comes to retirement savings once your debts are paid off!

We live in a society today where people where people want things no whether or not they can actually afford them. Instead of waiting until they have saved enough to purchase what they want, they instead purchase everything on credit.

Whenever you purchase something you don't have the money to pay for in full, you pay interest charges.

Credit card debt is one of the most dangerous and financially ruinous things you can have when it comes to not only saving for your retirement but also for purchasing everyday things in life today and tomorrow. You are essentially mortgaging your future when you buy things on credit. This does not mean that there is no place in life for credit cards or paying finance charges. It just means you have to use them carefully and wisely.

Think about what you might say if you walked into any store and the salesman told you the price of whatever you wanted to purchase was actually 12-18% higher than the price on the item itself. Would you buy it anyway or would you walk out? Most of us would walk out because there would be no way that we would pay 12-18% more than we were supposed to. That would just be common sense!

But when we purchase items on credit and don't pay them off COMPLETELY at the end of the billing cycle then you will be paying that extra 12-18% or even more with some credit cards! If you look at purchases from that point of view then you can easily see why purchasing on credit can be so dangerous!

If we grow up living within our means then we can get the most from the money we earn.

When we eliminate costly credit card finance charges we will have more money to go out and buy what we need or to save for our retirement or for other purchases. This is called living within our means and it is something that not enough people do today.

That is not to say that there is not a role in our lives for credit when used responsibly. Not many people have enough money to pay cash for an automobile and even fewer have the money to purchase a house with cash. For these types of purchases credit and a loan is an almost necessity. After all, you need transportation to get to work now so it is not reasonable for you to wait 3 years until you save up enough cash to purchase a car. And you need someplace warm and dry to sleep now not 5 years from now.

But when you need to take out a loan, pay careful attention to the interest rate, other fees, and payment terms. Once you get the loan, make every payment on time and try to pay it off faster if the interest rate is sufficiently high. Remember, any interest you pay the banks is money that you earned but have nothing to show for it. So make it your life's mission to give the banks and Uncle Sam as little as legally possible!

As you go through life, live a lifestyle that you will be able to afford. Don't buy a luxury car if you cannot afford it.

Don't purchase a huge house when a smaller one will do just fine. Don't take expensive luxury vacations if it means not being able to save for other things or pay other bills.

Think about purchases another way as well. There are purchases like houses and furniture and cars that you will have for several years or more. You will use them every day and they will make the quality of your life better. These are wise uses of your money as long as you keep the costs of these purchases in line with your income.

But then we have other purchases like going out to dinner, expensive wines, shows and other expenses that once you are done with them you have nothing to show for the money except for a memory or two. Though memories are important, and though you should spend some money enjoying yourself and life in general, remember that these purchases give you no long term benefit and you should think about how much money you spend on these kinds of purchases.

If you go out to eat 5 times a week and cannot save for your retirement, you had better remember how that steak tasted 30 years ago because you won't be buying steak anytime soon after you retire! Keep things in the proper perspective and live a balanced life where you take care of today in such a way that will also enable you to take care of tomorrow.

Be Realistic

Another area where many people find themselves getting into trouble is when they fail to look at life and retirement in realistic terms. Sometimes this comes from a feeling of entitlement and sometimes it comes from the expectation that things will be better shortly and we don't have to worry about the future. Both attitudes are wrong and can get you into a heck of a lot of trouble.

As far as how you live today, be realistic in what you can afford. Just because your neighbor has a boat or a beautiful house does not mean that you are entitled to one as well. If you can afford it, that is one thing. But if you believe that as long as someone else has something that you are entitled to it as well then you are dead wrong. That is entitlement and entitlement often results is a mountain of debt and financial ruin.

In terms of retirement planning, people often get into trouble when they are not realistic when it comes to what they are going to spend in retirement and what amount of money they need to live in a certain lifestyle. Underestimate either of those and you could be in for quite an unpleasant surprise late in life.

In retirement, expenses will change as compared to what you spent while you were working. For some people our expenses might be less and for others they might be more. For example, if your job includes a company vehicle and a company paid cell phone, then once you retire you will have to buy a car and pay for insurance and gas and repairs for that vehicle. You will also have to pay for your cell phone as well. Whether your expenses will be more or less is not the point. What is the point is that you understand what it is going to cost you live when you are retired.

Another area where people often misjudge is that they think that whatever something costs today that is what it will cost 10 or 20 years from now. The reality is that although some things may stay the same almost everything else is going to go up. Some things more than others but there will be price increases.

Rent and property tax are sure to go up. Food and clothing will go up. Medical costs will be much higher. You need to be realistic when you decide what you are going to need to live each month. You can overestimate and have money left over and that will be good.

But if you under estimate than you might wind up going through all your savings and still have several years left to live!

My advice to you is to contact one of the financial investment firms or speak to a financial advisor and find out what inflation rates they are using for people your age when it comes to living expense forecasts.

Once you know that you can more accurately see what you should have when it comes to a yearly retirement living allowance.

But even when you get the supposed accurate inflation number always plan on saving more so you will have a little bit more. Inflation estimates are exactly that. They are estimates. They can be accurate or they can be way off. It is better to have a little bit more and live well than to plan on the minimum and then fall short.

Another factor might be where you plan on living when you retire. Are you going to stay where you are now or are you going to move? If you are going to move, where would you move to? Would the cost of living there be higher or lower than where you currently are? Will there be a state income tax or not? Will insurance costs be higher or lower?

There are a lot of factors to consider when it comes to the amount of money you think you will need. Be honest with yourself and be realistic about your future expenses.

No one has ever complained about having too much money at the end of the year. But a lot of people become upset when they outlive their savings.

Do these forecasts as early as you can. Remember these are only estimates to be used to determine how much you need to save now in order to make those estimates become a reality for you. You can always change your forecasts as you and your lives change. Nothing is set in stone. But you need something to get your plan started so start forecasting now and refine that forecast as you go along.

Pay Yourself Not Uncle Sam!

In most households there is a limited amount of money coming in every month. By that I mean we have certain salaries or commission income that varies little or not at all. So we have to take steps to get as much value from that money as possible. Then, we are able to save more for our retirement and other things. One of the ways we can get more money is by limiting the amount we pay in taxes every year.

Taxes are a necessary evil in this world. Everything the government does, both good and bad, and provides to us has to be paid from somewhere and that "somewhere" comes from our pocketbooks in the form of taxes. But that doesn't mean we should not look for ways to reduce the amount of taxes we pay each year to the absolute minimum.

Notice I said "reduce" the amount of taxes and not that we should avoid paying taxes. That would be illegal and result in penalties that would exceed the amount we saved anyway.

We need to pay our fair share and all that we are supposed to pay but not anymore. We can do that in a number of ways.

We can take advantage of pre-tax retirement savings programs such as 401K accounts and IRA accounts and other types of pre-tax savings plans available through our employers. These are great because they take your money out before taxes are figured so you wind up saving more than it really costs you. For example, saving $100 before tax actually only costs you around $70 depending on your tax rate. So you wind up saving more and paying less in taxes.

Another way to make sure that you are paying only your fair share and nothing more is to hire someone reputable to prepare your taxes for you. The more complex your tax return is the more likely it will be that you will make a mistake or miss an important deduction or two. This can cost you a lot of money. If you were to take a look at the tax code, you would quickly realize that there is so much to know and learn that you and I would never be able to do as good a job as a licensed tax professional.

A licensed tax professional, if qualified, might also be able to advise you on things you can do moving forward that would lessen your tax burden and enable you to pay less taxes moving forward.

This will put more money in your pocket and make it easier for you to save more with less impact on your lifestyle.

The thing about taxes is that you pay thousands of dollars every year and don't really get anything tangible or real in exchange for that money.

Yes, you get services and the use of our infrastructure but you don't get products or food or housing from those tax payments.

Taxes come in many forms in addition to income tax. We have property taxes if you own a home, we pay sales tax, gas tax, mortgage taxes and a whole slew of other taxes buried in the fine print on many things we purchase every year. If there is a way to reduce those taxes it puts more money in your pocket.

As far as property taxes are concerned you might be able to file a grievance if you feel your taxes are too high. There are firms that fight these cases for you in exchange for a percentage of the first year savings. Then you pocket the savings every year moving forward. If you save $1,000 on your property taxes that would be $1,000 for your retirement savings with no impact on your lifestyle!

The whole idea is to limit those expenses that give us nothing tangible in return. Tax payments and any kind of interest are prime examples.

So take a look at your tax situation and see if there are any ways where you can reduce your tax and interest payments and channel those funds into your retirement savings instead.

The result is more money for retirement with no negative effect on your standard of living or lifestyle.

Invest Wisely & Responsibly

We all like to get as much for our money as possible. We want the lowest price for the largest size. We want value and we want savings. There is nothing wrong with that approach and usually it is the best approach to take except when it makes us throw common sense out the window and invest foolishly.

Unfortunately there are people in this world who exist solely to separate you from your money. They prey on the weak or uninformed and they really prey on the greedy. Their sales pitches are finely crafted to get people like you and I to give them our hard earned money and never see most or all of it again.

These people look like you and I. In fact, many of them look better than you and I. they wear expense suits, have beautiful offices and just look like they are very successful and knowledgeable. But this is all part of the process designed to impress you so that you don't look too close to what they are selling.

Let me say right up front that I am by no means an investment expert. In fact, I would say that there are a ton of people more qualified to talk to you about investments than I. But I do have a ton of common sense and often that is all you need to have in order to know when to stand up and run like hell out the door before they take your money.

With that in mind, here are a few things you should always look for when it comes to investing your retirement savings or any other kind of savings:

The old saying that if it sounds too good to be true then it probably isn't really applies to investing. It is amazing when you hear about all these scams and pyramid schemes out there that people actually invested with these crooks. If someone told me that when banks are paying 2% and stocks are paying 10% that they can get me 30% on my money, that would make my eyes open and warning flags shoot through my head.

But that is exactly what made people give their hard earned money to these people. Poor people gave their life savings in search of the holy grail of investments. People lost their entire retirement savings when they were just a few years away from needing that money! So if someone is guaranteeing you enormous interest rates much, much higher than you can get anywhere else, please think twice, no wait, think 5 times before investing.

Second, never invest more than you can afford to lose. Even if an investment looks good and is proven legitimate, remember that all stock investments can go up but they can also go down. No stock is a guaranteed winner so if you think something is a really good opportunity, go ahead and invest but no more than you could afford to lose if the company goes under.

Third, because of the unsure nature of individual stocks, diversify your investments. Don't put all your money in one company or stock. Spread it around in several different companies or markets so if one should go down the others will help stabilize your investment. You might want to have some money is stocks, some in bonds and other investments.

Fourth, be careful with start-up company stocks. Though they sometimes have the best chance of paying off really well, they also have the best chance of going under and you losing everything. These investments can be very risky. Invest a little if you feel it is a good investment but be careful.

Fifth, some investments are more risky than others. If you have 40 years before you retire you have a chance to recoup anything that is lost short-term or to recover from a total loss. But if you are a year or two away from retirement, think about investing in more stable and secure investments.

After all, if you lose half your money when you are retired you cannot easily replace it or wait for the stocks to come back!

If a stock broker or investment counselor contacts you with an offer, be very careful. Who knows where they got your name and who knows if they are legitimate or not. They might be running a scam or some other game and you are the target. Check them out through independent resources. Don't use their references as they are probably part of the scam. Better yet, rely on people recommended by people you trust or who are associated with well-known and respected firms. Even this is not always a guaranteed success but at least you will have done your homework and made a wise decision when you made it.

Last, but certainly not least, if someone tells you that you have to invest NOW and once you walk out the door the opportunity will not be available to you, run for the hills. This is the "time share" approach. They do not want you to leave and have the opportunity to check them out or investigate their company or opportunity. They don't want that because they know you will uncover information that shows this is not something you should invest in or purchase.

Last, but certainly not least, check out every counselor or company with your local consumer affairs or Better Business Bureau to see if there are any complaints against them. At least this will give you a heads up before you risk any of your money.

People will complain to help save people like you and I from making the same mistakes they made.

Conversely, if you do make a mistake and get ripped off, report the person and the company. There not only might be a chance of recovering part of your investment but you might help someone else avoid making the same mistake you made and losing their money as well. You would like someone to do that for you so it makes sense that you should do the same thing for them.

Lower Rates Means More Savings!

This one is really simple. If you have to borrow money for any reason, take the time to shop around for the lowest rates and the best deals. Just one or two percentage points can make a huge difference in the amount of interest you will pay the banks or financial institutions. Since we get nothing tangible for our interest payments, it just makes sense to pay as little interest as possible.

Credit cards can carry interest rates anywhere from 9% to over 30%! That is a HUGE difference and can easily result in thousands of extra dollars in interest payments! Read the fine print and shop around for the best deals. If your credit rating is good you will probably qualify for one of the lower interest cards. If your credit rating is poor then you probably will have to get one of the higher interest rate cards. If that is your case, pay them off as quickly as possible.

Mortgage and car loans are the same way. For every zero interest loan at one dealer there is a 12% loan at another.

Even though the price of the car might be a little lower, the interest paid will more than offset that and cost you hundreds of dollars extra over the cost of the loan! Do your homeowner and read the fine print. Compare the dealership loans with the loan you could get from your bank or credit union and choose the best deal.

The best way to use credit cards is to pay your bills off in full when the statement comes. This way you get the flexibility of using the card and being able to purchase things without carrying around large amounts of money. Not only that but credit cards have theft protection and other benefits built into them. As long as you can pay the bill in full every month, you will be good to go!

I also advise using a card that gives you some kind of added benefit in the form of a rewards program where you earn cash back or airline miles or some other tangible benefit. If you pay your bill in full you will wind up getting these benefits and perks for free! My wife and I, for example, have taken 6 trips to Hawaii for free! All from credit card airline miles!

Sometimes, especially in the case of auto loans and home mortgages, you simply cannot afford to pay off the loan in one month. In these cases, make sure you get a loan with no pre-payment penalty. That means you can pay extra every month to reduce the amount you owe. This enables you to reduce the interest payments as well.

Doing this can turn a 5 year car loan into a 3 or 4 year loan.

You can turn a 30 year mortgage into a 15 year mortgage as well! This gives you the flexibility of smaller monthly payment but allows you to pay more when you are able to. You can easily save hundreds or thousands of dollars using this simple method!

One important thing is to forget about paying the minimum payment the credit card companies say is all you need to pay each month. If you adhere to that schedule you will take years and years to pay off one purchase and you would wind up paying thousands of dollars in interest! Make every effort to pay off credit card debt as quickly as possible. If you are saddled with several credit card bills, or have a large amount of credit card debt, consider consolidating all those debts into one larger debt paid off by a low interest loan.

For example, if you have $20,000 in credit card debt at 18% interest, the interest payments will be crushing. But if you can take that debt and pay it off with a home equity or personal loan at 5% you will save a ton of money. Just do not run up more credit card debt at the same time because you now have a zero balance on those accounts!

Also be aware that you should not suspend your retirement savings while paying down debt unless your interest rates are very high and it makes sense to do so. You should keep your company retirement plan funded to keep the company match intact. Never give up free money your employer offers you.

If you do have debt, I strongly suggest talking to a financial planner or to one of the free debt counselling programs available to consumers. They will help you decide on the best way to pay off the debt and get you back on track. They will also help you stay on track by teaching you how to use credit better in the future.

The 100 Plan

Hey, I've got great news for you! People are living longer now than ever before! Advances in medical care and healthy living have increased the number of years we can expect on living! Isn't that great news! Of course it is!

But this also means that your retirement savings will have to last you longer than your parents or grandfathers saving had to last them. If you plan to live to 100 and retire at 65, then you have to be able to find your retirement for 35 years! That means you have a nice amount of money to save!

While this doesn't mean you are going to live to be 100, it does mean that you cannot count of living only until you are just 85 and only have to worry about paying for 20 years of retirement. If you plan on funding 20 years of retirement and wind up needing 35 years of funding you will be in bad shape!

One of the unfair things about retirement planning is that we have no idea how long we are going to be alive in retirement or what our physical condition is going to be during the last years of our lives.

So we need to plan for the long-term and understand that we might need more than less money. While the perfect retirement nest egg would run out the day after we pass on, the reality is that some of us will die with money in the bank while other will run out long before they pass on.

It used to be that the retirement models used by financial advisors planned on 25-30 years of retirement. While those are still good indications of what you might need, many people are using the 100 year old baseline now because it offers more protection and more conservative measure of retirement needs.

So what does this mean to you and I? Well it means that we are going to live longer but we are going to have to save more because the longer we are around the more things are going to cost and the more medical care we are going to need. It is not just that we are going to be around longer, it is going to be that things are going to cost more at the end of our lifespan as well.

Think about that for a moment. If inflation is just at 3% a year and we are possibly going to be around 5 -10 years longer, then near the end of our years we can expect things to cost another 15-30% at that time. When everything costs 15-30% more, we are going to need 15-30% more just to keep up.

We are not saying this to frighten you but instead to impress upon you the need to forecast your needs accurately and early in the saving process so you know what you are going to need. If you use the data that your mom and dad used or told you about, you might be setting yourself up for coming up short in your savings.

Take a look at your family history. Do most or all of your relatives live long and healthy lives? Did grandpa live to be 95 and grandma live to be 100? What about mom and dad? Did they live into their late 80's or 90's? If they did then you have every right to expect to live that long or longer as well and you need to factor that into your retirement plan.

Also consider your overall health now. Are you disease free and in good health and in good shape? If so, that is great! But if you are not in good health or in good shape perhaps this would be a good time to change some habits and make some new resolutions for your future.

Living to 100 is not a right but something that you can influence by what you do today. Lose some weight, get in shape and eat healthier too. If you are going to save all that retirement money you just might want to be around as long as you can to spend it. Your kids would rather have you around than your money.

Medical Costs

Medical costs are the big question mark when it comes to saving for retirement. Just like no one knows how long they are going to live, no one knows what kind of medical treatment they are going to need as they grow older either. And with medical costs going through the roof today, they can eat up a lot of your retirement savings very quickly.

Some people estimate that a reasonably healthy couple will need roughly $200 – 250,000 over the course of their retirement just to pay for health care or health care insurance premiums! While you might not need that much, you should be aware that health care is a real cost for retirees and you need to deal with that.

Medicare will cover the cost of some health care but many people elect to purchase supplemental medical coverage to provide better or enhanced coverage for other medical issues or to provide a better level of care with more options. Like anything else in life, anything that provides more or better of something is going to cost you money.

Cost of insurance is going to depend largely upon your age and your overall health. I would suggest discussing your future needs to your insurance agent or medical professional so you can get an idea of what your costs are likely to be. But keep in mind that any costs you are given today will only estimates and they can change significantly over time.

Other insurance you might wish to consider is long term insurance that will provide coverage for assisted living or nursing home care should you or your partner require that. With skilled care facilities getting anywhere from $5,000 - $20,000 a MONTH, that can burn through your savings very quickly!

Don't overlook medical care costs when you figure out your retirement needs. This is one area where many people fail to adequately plan for and it can place your entire retirement plan in jeopardy.

Your Credit Rating

Let's stop looking at the future for a moment even though this has everything to do with your future. When we talk about credit ratings, we are talking about how companies look at you as far as their overall risk in lending you money or providing you with a line of credit or a credit card. The better your credit rating, the better risk you are and the more options that will become available for you.

People think it is easy to get credit these days and they are right. It is TOO easy to get credit. Just about anyone can get a credit card or a loan these days and that gets a lot of people in trouble. People who abuse credit often find themselves up to their ears in debt.

But although it is easy to get credit, it is not that easy to get GOOD credit. Loan rates and interest rates are very dependent on your credit rating. A person with a good credit rating might get a 3% loan while a person with bad credit might get a 10% loan from the same company. Same company, same money but at over 3 times the interest rate!

That is because people with poor credit ratings are more likely to default or be late with payments. So while they can get the money, they pay through the nose for it in the form of higher interest rates.

A good credit rate not only saves you money but makes it easier to get better financial opportunities and lower rates on a wide variety of financial products from insurance to mortgages and auto loans. But when it comes to retirement, credit ratings can become even more important.

Getting credit when you are retired can be difficult because unlike people who are employed, retired people have limited ways to earn money to repay their loans. So their credit applications are looked at differently and with a different set of guidelines. A retired person with a good credit rating or credit score will be able to get more and do more than the same person with a bad credit rating.

I urge everyone reading this book to get a free copy of their credit scores at least once a year. There are services that you can go to and get this information for free. Check the report, look at your scores and make sure they are the highest they can be. If you have any negative entries or issues then address them and try and get them resolved and removed. Work on getting your score to the highest it can be. It will save you money in the long run.

If you have any overdue or delinquent accounts, contact each account and work out a plan to pay those debts off. Do not ignore them and think that they will go away because they won't. Don't think that bankruptcy is an easy way out either regardless of what those commercials might tell you. Declaring bankruptcy today can ruin your credit for a long time.

If your credit history is really bad, or if you have credit problems now, consider talking to a credit counsellor who can advise you on the best way to work yourself out of trouble. They can often contact your creditors in your behalf and work out payment plans. In some cases they can reduce your debt or help you consolidate it. However you accomplish it, take care of your credit problems as quickly as you can so you can take steps to rebuild your credit profile and history.

Close accounts you have that are open but that you never use anymore. Even though they have a zero balance they can still work against you because you still have access to that credit line. So those 47 accounts you opened up over the years to get a free toaster or airline ticket can work against you now. Look over your credit report and clean it up. Keep what you use and close the other accounts.

Also look for entries and inquiries that you know nothing about. People often will steal other people's identities and open up credit card accounts in other people's names. You might have your credit rating destroyed by other people without your knowledge.

Another problem is that as you get closer to retirement you become more at risk for fraudulent behavior. People target the elderly or older people because they are less likely to understand exactly what is going on. They are more vulnerable and easier to manipulate. Checking your credit score every year will help you discover fraudulent activity faster and earlier and limit the damage it can do.

Going into your retirement with an exceptionally higher credit rating is one of the smartest things anyone can do. It will help you manage your finances more easily and effectively while making it easier to maintain your lifestyle at the same time. We need credit to survive and we need a good credit rating to get it!

Retirement is a Work in Progress

So far in the first part of this book we have talked about the attitudes regarding retirement saving and the things we need to do in order to best prepare us for our retirement. But we must also realize that what we do today is going to change over time. Retirement planning is not something we do today and then forget about it until we hit 65.

Retirement plans are constantly changing. We may move investments or change the amount of savings. We may change our approach when it comes to insurances and medical needs. Our goals might change or we might have an event in our lives that takes our entire plan and turns it upside down!

Whatever the reasons might be, we need to constantly take out our retirement plan and see if it still makes sense to us and is still a valid and effective plan. Usually we might make a minor change or tweak or two and keep things pretty much where they were. Very rarely do we have to blow the whole thing up and start all over. (This assumes we made a pretty good plan in the first place!)

Life changes around us every day. Prices change, investments change, inflation changes, health changes and we as individuals change as well. Sometimes what we thought we wanted to do in retirement turns out not to be what we want as we got closer. Maybe the beach is Hawaii is not what we want now because we can't stand the heat as we got older and now a home on the lake looks better!

Like we said, things change.

As long as we keep our retirement plans up to date and they are based on honesty and reality we should do just fine. At least as best as we possibly can be because no one can see into the future. The only thing we can do now is to do the best we can when it comes to planning our future. Then we have to sit back and see how accurately we forecasted things and make adjustments as they are needed.

Our goal should be to enjoy the latter years of our life and we can only do that when we have enough money to live without constant worrying. We don't need a beach front home to be happy but we must have peace of mind and confidence in our ability to provide for our immediate and long-range future. So plan for later, save now for later and keep your fingers on the pulse of your retirement plans. Make changes as they are needed and you should do just fine.

So now that we have covered the attitudes and the basics of financial planning and security, let's take a look at some of the easy ways we can turn our retirement dreams into our retirement reality. You may not need them all but you will undoubtedly need some of them.

26 Ways Anyone Can Save for their Retirement

1. Play the Match Game!

Anytime your company will give you money for saving towards your retirement, take advantage of it! This is like free money over and above what you earn in salary and benefits. Accepting matching money will help you grow your retirement nest egg faster with less effort and less change to your lifestyle and with less sacrifice.

Some companies will match you either on a dollar for dollar basis or a percentage basis up to certain limits. For example, a company might match the first 3% of your salary that you contribute to your 401K. So if you earn $100,000 a year and contribute $3,000 to your 401K, the company will add $3,000 to your contribution.

In that example you have used just $3,000 of you money but received a $3,000 bonus and now have $6,000 in your 401K. But if you only contributed $1,500 you would only get $1,500 from the company and not the $3,000 max matching contribution.

Taking advantage of the company matching program is the single greatest way to get the most for your retirement. If you are not currently signed up for this program and your company offers it, sign up for it tomorrow and then contribute enough to get the full matching contribution if at all possible.

This is also a benefit that you should look for if you are considering changing jobs. Since the matching contribution is essentially a raise, it must not be overlooked when evaluating total compensation packages.

If your company does not offer a matching contribution program, why not ask if they would consider doing so? You really have nothing to lose and a whole lot to gain.

2. Even a Little Means a Lot

One of the most common misconceptions when it comes to saving is that you must save a lot every month in order to make an impact on your savings. This is not only false, it is a dangerous view to take of the savings process.

Earlier we used an example where someone could only contribute $100 a year. That is just a little less than $2 a week. About half the price of a latte or coffee these days. But even $100 a year for ten years gives you over $1,000 plus all the interest you would have earned.

But if you had not saved anything because you thought it wouldn't matter, you would have exactly nothing in your savings plus you would have earned no interest. Even the most clueless person should be able to see the wisdom in saving any amount of money no matter how small.

Think about it another way. Depending on the interest rate you get, whatever you do save will double itself in anywhere from 7 to 15 years.

So if you saved $100 a month back when you were 20 and just did that for one year, you would have $4,000 to over $8,000 in savings when you hit 65 even if you never added another penny to your original $1,000!

The point is, save whenever you can and however much you can. Even if it is only pennies, those pennies can add up. Something is always better than nothing. You can build on something but you cannot build on nothing.

So figure out what you can put aside. I don't care if it is just 10 bucks. Take that 10 bucks and put it in an account and let it grow. If you do this enough times over the course of your employed years, you can make a nice difference in retirement.

So come on, start something. Even if it is just a little something……..

3. Pay Yourself First

As we go through life there will always be things to spend money on and excuses for not saving here or there. There will always be something more important or something you want more. Eventually, as you constantly make excuses and consistently avoid saving you find yourself getting older and grayer with nothing in the bank.

Savings is one area where good intentions don't mean very much. You might want to save and you might intend to save but if at the end of the year you haven't saved there will be no money in the bank.

The best way to save is to pay yourself first and then pay your bills and expenses with what is left over. Utilize payroll deduction so you never see the money in the first place. Take that retirement contribution and get it socked away before you ever see it. That is one of the easiest and most effective ways to save.

Any time you get some extra money take a portion of it and save it before you get a chance to spend it on something else. Paying yourself first is a great way to force yourself to save.

4. Payroll Deduction

When we get our paycheck, we look at the amount and that is what we use to pay our bills and determine what we can afford and what has to be postponed. If that check already has some retirement savings taken out of it we will never see it or miss it. All we will have at the end of the year is a year's worth of contributions. Not 11 month's or 8 month's but a full year's worth of deposits! Over the years that will add up for you!

Direct deposit or payroll deduction helps us make scheduled deposits without being tempted to spend the money on something else. Again, it doesn't have to be a huge deduction to start. Do what you can and what you can sustain. You can always add to those deposits when you have a little bit of extra cash at the end of the month. As things improve for you financially you might consider increasing those monthly deposits as you can afford them.

Another important reason for payroll deduction or direct deposit is that it takes away the effort and the need to remember to make those deposits into our savings plans. They just happen automatically and we don't have to do a darned thing to make them continue. It is kind of auto-pilot savings for your retirement or other savings need.

In short, payroll deduction or direct deposit helps make savings easier and any time something is easier we tend to stay with it longer and have greater levels of success. I mean why take a more difficult route when there is an easier alternative.

Almost every employer today has some form of direct deposit or payroll deduction. Almost all retirement fund companies offer direct deposit or scheduled transfers as well. Contact them and set up your automatic investment plan today. Even if it is just a few dollars a month, get started now. We have already talked about how just a few dollars can easily add up to thousands when retirement rolls around.

5. Pre-Tax Bliss

We already discussed this in broader terms in our first section of the book but pre-tax savings allow you to deposit more money into your retirement accounts with less impact on your lifestyle. It is definitely one of the most important ways for you to save for retirement.

The usual pre-tax savings vehicles are 401K and other company sponsored retirement accounts. If your company offers one of these types of retirement plans then sign up and have your deduction taken out as a pre-tax deduction. This allows you to avoid paying taxes on the money you are saving.

For example, if you are in a 30% tax bracket, saving $100 would only "cost" you $70 because you would be avoiding paying the taxes on that $100. So you would be saving $100 into your account but your paycheck would only be $70 less. This might not sound like a lot of money but when you save thousands each year you can save thousands as well!

Keep in mind that there are limits as to how much you can put away every year into these accounts. You cannot simply dump your whole check into retirement and avoid paying any taxes. These limits increase as you get close to retirement so check with your plan administrator or the company where your accounts are located to get the current limits and other details.

In addition, you might be eligible to open up a self-directed account called an IRS (Individual Retirement Account) where you can save for retirement if you do not have a company sponsored retirement plan. These deposits can be deducted from your income tax form when you prepare it and lessen the amount of tax due.

Regardless of what plan you use, saving money pre-tax enables you to save more money in less time with less impact on your lifestyle. There are some tax considerations you might have to deal with depending on your income now and your projected income when you are retired.

Since all of the amount in your retirement account will be taxable when you retire, you will have to pay taxes as you withdraw the money from your accounts. But since most people have a lower tax rate during retirement this is still a better option. If you will be in a higher tax bracket during retirement saving via pre-tax might not be a good deal for you. Something that is tax free in retirement such as a ROTH IRA might be a better choice.

Contact your accountant or financial advisor to see what the best options are for you.

6. Post Tax Blast

OK, this might not apply to everyone reading this but if you are able to save more than you are allowed to deposit into your retirement accounts, there is no law or regulation that prohibits you from saving more in conventional savings accounts. This may come in handy as you get closer to retirement and discover you are short of your goals.

Talk to your plan administrator to see what your plan limits are for your plan and at your age. Age does sometimes play a role as older people are allowed an extra "catch-up" deduction. But even if you have reached your limit, there may be other options open to you.

You may be able to contribute to a regular IRA or a ROTH IRA depending on your own situation. Again, check with your plan administrator to see if you are eligible for these savings accounts as well. If you are eligible then you will be able to increase your savings amounts by opening one of those accounts as well.

You can also purchase stocks, bonds, Certificates of Deposit at your local bank, or just open up a good old fashion savings account to sock some money away in. Just be aware that savings accounts today do not pay very much in the way of interest so those should be your last resort. But any way you can save money is better than not saving at all.

If you have considerable resources to dedicate to your retirement, or if you have a one year windfall, then discuss the best options for investing those funds with your financial planner or advisor. Limits are only for certain accounts and there will always be other methods of investing open to you.

7. Split that Raise

One very easy way to save money for your retirement without sacrificing very much or suffering is to take every raise or bonus you get and dedicate some or all of it towards your retirement. After all, these funds are something that you have not become "used to" yet so you can sock them away without feeling much of the impact.

Let's say that you get a $500 a month salary increase and that increase works out to be $300 after taxes. Well, you can take that $300 and do a payroll deduction or direct deposit into your retirement account. This way you will continue to pay your expenses off your "old" salary just like you never received the raise. But your retirement account will grow accordingly.

If you cannot save the entire amount, that is OK as well. After all, everything goes up these days and we usually need at least some kind of increase to help keep pace with the economy. So if you have that $300 extra in your monthly income now, then take $100 or $200 and save that while using the rest for expenses.

Any time we take money and save it before we become accustomed to it, we make it easier to save money. But, and this is a big but, if you NEED that money to pay bills and expenses, you may not be able to save it no matter how much you might want to. One thing you do not want to do is save that extra money and then have to go into debt and pay high credit card interest rates. If you do that, you will wind up behind as debt piles up.

You can also do the same thing with unexpected or one time payments such as bonuses, inheritances, etc. Or. If you get a lot of overtime one week, take a portion of that and save it. If you really want to, you can find ways to save a few dollars here and a few dollars there.

8. Tax Refund Boost

Every year people get millions of dollars in income tax refunds. Why not take that refund and instead of spending it on a nice vacation or a new car or sound system, why not use it to boost that retirement savings account?

Tax refunds are a one-time source of cash for some people but they fail to utilize that opportunity to its full extent. Use the same approach as we just talked about with raises or bonuses. You don't have to save the entire refund if you have a need for some of it. But anything you can put away will help make your retirement savings grow even faster.

Some people intentionally have more money taken out of each check as a kind of forced savings. They then use the refund to make a large purchase when they get it. If you are going to use that refund as a savings boost, consider paying in less every week and instead transferring that amount to your savings instead.

When you have money sitting in your tax account with the government, you are essentially giving them the use of your money for the entire year without them giving you any interest on that money. So your money is working for them not for you! If you are getting large refunds every year, then contribute less each week and do a direct deposit instead. But when you do get that refund, invest it in your future.

9. Bonus Time Bonanza!

Some of us get bonuses at certain times of the year. This is money over and above our regular salary. We get those bonuses either at the end of the year or several times throughout the year. Whatever your schedule might be, take advantage of it!

Some people use their bonuses as their total retirement deposit every year and there is nothing wrong with that. If your 401K limit is $15,000 and your bonus is equal to that or more, then funding your retirement account for that year is easy! You don't even miss the money because you never saw it in the first place.

The one problem with that approach though is that if your bonus is paid at the end of the year, you miss out on the interest that money would have earned during that year if you had made weekly or monthly deposits. With that in mind you would have more money if you made regular payments equaling the same amount throughout the year instead of doing a lump sum deposit in late December.

If your bonus is paid in January or February, you would then have those funds invested for the full year.

You can do the same thing with any type of bonus or rewards you might receive throughout the year. Investing extra money is always easier than taking money out of every paycheck you get throughout the year. Keep in mind that missing just one weekly or monthly payment during the year would wipe out any advantage of investing throughout the year as opposed to the one payment.

10. Mortgage Muscle

For most of us, our home mortgage is our largest debt and our largest monthly payment. Not only are the payments large in size, they are also the longest lasting payments you will ever make as well. With most mortgages today going for 15-30 years, any savings we can make on that debt will help us have more money left over for retirement.

You can save money on mortgages in several different ways. Here are just a couple of ways you can either reduce interest payments or your monthly payments or both:

First and foremost, you want to get the lowest interest rates as possible. If you are looking for a new home search very hard for the lowest rates and fees possible so that you get the very best overall deal on your new home. Even a tenth or a percent difference can be worth 10's of thousands of dollars over the cost of the loan.

Check with banks, private lenders, credit unions and any other source of home mortgages. If you currently have a bank that you use for savings and checking then perhaps getting a mortgage with that institution will qualify you for a special or lower rate. Sometimes you can save money by having your payments done by direct deposit instead of paying them manually every month. Anything you can do to get a lower rate should be looked into very carefully.

If you currently have a high interest mortgage, you may want to look into refinancing your current mortgage and taking advantage of the lower interest rates. But keep in mind that there are fees and taxes involved in doing so and these will be out of pocket costs. You might be able to roll over those costs into the new loan and still wind up with a lower monthly payment or shorter term loan.

If you think this might make sense for you, talk to your financial advisor. Do NOT ask the people offering the loans if refinancing is a good idea for you. Some of them are just interested in selling their loans and might not act or advise in your best interests. But if the rate difference is several percentage points or more, you should really look into this as it could save you a lot of money.

Second, the term or length of the loan is important as well. If you can afford the payments on a 15 year loan instead of a 30 year loan, you will save a TON of money! Getting the shortest term that has payments that you can afford is usually the best way to go. But if you cannot afford the payments and will have to rely heavily on credit, think again about getting a longer term loan.

Also, if you will not be able to save for your retirement with a shorter term loan because of the higher payments, think carefully about that. Don't fall into the trap of telling yourself that you will catch up later after the loan is paid off. There will always be other things to buy, college educations to pay for and other expenses. Create an entire budget, including mortgage and retirement savings now rather than wait until later.

Another option you may have available to you might be to pay slightly larger payments every month that go directly to the principal on the loan. Check to see if your mortgage allows you to pre-pay off the loan without a penalty. This can be especially useful at the start of the loan when most of your payments go towards interest.

For example, depending on your individual loan, making the equivalent of one extra payment in a year could shorten the loan by a full year in the first few years of the loan! You could very well turn a 30 year mortgage into a 15 or 20 year loan just by making small extra payments throughout the year!

The advantage of doing this is that your required monthly payment would still be lower so you could still pay the standard payment when you had to but could make the larger payments when you were able to. This would enable you to pay off the loan earlier, save a ton of interest money while keeping your credit rating intact as well.

Keep in mind that as of the writing of this book mortgage interest was tax deductible. So paying off the loan earlier would lessen your overall mortgage interest deduction. The vast majority of us will still do better paying off the loan earlier but if you have any doubts, talk to a financial advisor to see if this makes sense for you in your situation.

In order for any of this to help you save for retirement assumes that you would use the interest savings to enable you to save this extra money towards your retirement. If you go out and buy a luxury car when your mortgage is over because you no longer have that monthly mortgage payment that would defeat the purpose of what you had been doing as far as retirement is concerned.

Any time you can reduce the cost of interest on any debt, you will free up more money to be used for other purposes. Like saving more towards your retirement.

11. Minimize Fees

Fees are just other expenses that cost you money without giving you anything tangible in return. When it comes to retirement plans and savings options, fees take on an entire new meaning that you should be very aware of and concerned about.

Whenever you have retirement accounts that involve mutual funds or stock funds, there might be fees paid to administrate those funds for you. Those fees pay for the people who manage the funds and make the trades and purchases that help make those funds profitable. But someone has to pay those people's salaries and that someone is you!

Fees can vary widely and these fees are some of the ways people make a killing getting people to invest with them and their funds. You could pay one half percent fees on one account while another account or fund might have a 5% fee! These fees come right off our investment profit or loss for the year. Even when a fund loses money the fund still gets their fee!

Whenever you are investing, ask to see the prospectus on the accounts or funds you are considering investing in. Look specifically for the fees and other charges that you will have to pay if you purchase those funds. Don't be fooled by what might appear to be a small percentage. Remember that 1% of $100,000 is still $1,000 that you will pay every year from your earnings! If you are fortunate enough to have $1,000,000 invested then that same 1% would mean a $10,000 fee!

There are "no-load" funds that do not charge fees and these might be good choices for you. But remember that fund managers and the companies they work for have to make money as well so there might be other charges or fees hidden in there somewhere. Ask very pointedly about all fees and charges and then monitor your account statements monthly to make sure nothing else is being charged to your accounts.

Let me say at this point that investing considerable amounts of money in stocks, bonds and funds requires a lot of knowledge. That is why it is important to have a person or company that is reputable and who you can trust with your savings. But even if you have the most trustworthy person and company in the world, you still need to be aware of what is going on in your account.

12. Reduce High Cost Interest

We have already talked about mortgage interest so now let's discuss other forms of interest that we must pay.

Generally, anything that we purchase that we cannot pay for in full will cost us some form of interest payment. Sometimes there are exceptions but even in those exceptions there may be conditions that have to be met to avoid paying interest.

Naturally, the best way to reduce the high cost of interest is to not pay interest in the first place. Pay off your credit card bill in full every month before the due date. Save up for larger purchases and live within your means. If you adopt this philosophy then you won't have to worry too much about interest rates.

But for some of us, interest is a part of life and we cannot avoid it. Large purchases like automobiles often require loans and loans have interest rates. So with that in mind, here are a few ways you can reduce the amount of money you pay in interest and increase the amount of money you will have to save for retirement:

First and foremost, search for the lowest interest rates available when it comes to credit cards and personal or automobile loans. Even a tenth or a percent can add significant interest to your monthly payments. Look at the credit disclosure on EVERY credit card account you have. If any of those accounts are higher than the others, think about either using a different payment method or shopping elsewhere. Every penny you pay in interest is a penny that you get nothing in return for.

If your cards have high rates, search for replacement cards that offer lower rates. This can save you a lot of money while still giving you the convenience of paying using a credit card. You would be surprised how different rates can be on very similar cards.

Second, if you have credit card debt, pay it off as quickly as you can. Forget the minimum monthly payment that is on your bill. If you just pay that your balance will never be paid off! Pay as much as you can and get that credit card balance back to zero. If you have multiple credit cards with balances on them, pay the accounts with the higher interest rates off first. Those are the one strangling you with interest charges.

Third, if you have credit card debt, consider putting all your credit cards except one in your safe deposit box so you cannot get to them. Keep one for emergencies and for places such as car rental agencies where credit cards are required. Making higher monthly payments to reduce balances will not work if you continue to overuse those cards at the same time. Pay cash or don't buy.

Fourth, credit card interest rates are extremely high compared to other forms of credit. You might want to consider taking all your credit card debt and their 18-30% interest and combining them into one personal loan at a much lower interest rate. This will result in paying less interest and enabling you to pay off your debt faster and cheaper. But this will not work if you keep overusing your cards after you consolidate your debt. Until everything is paid off, pay by cash or don't buy.

Do a financial and credit "audit" on yourself every 6 month to a year. Examine your credit accounts and see what their current interest rates are and what their terms are. If there are other options available to you then take advantage of those options. Credit card companies are fighting amongst each other for your business. So you could wind up the winner in the form of lower interest rates.

But regardless of whether you have credit card debt or other loan debt, one thing every form of credit or loan will have in common will be your credit rating.

Having a higher credit rating or score will help go a long way in qualifying you for the lowest interest rates possible. Credit card companies like people with high credit scores because those people have shown a history of paying their bills on time and rarely defaulting. Which means the credit card companies lose less when they give credit to those people.

People with high credit ratings are the ones every credit card company targets for new lower interest credit card accounts. So you will be doing yourself a huge favor by protecting your credit history and credit scores.

Another thing to be careful with when it comes to credit cards is making what the industry calls "impulse buys". These are purchases that people make because they are easy to make and they get caught up in the moment. If they didn't have the cash and had to leave and come back, most of these purchase would never be made. So be careful and don't buy things just because it is easy. If you need it and can afford it, then buy it. Otherwise, pass it by.

You might be wondering why we are talking so much about credit cards in a book on retirement savings. Well, the more money we spend on interest and servicing credit card debt the less we have to dedicate to the really important things in life such as saving for retirement. Most of us have a limited amount of money coming in every month and when we pay a considerable amount of that on interest that leaves us much less for everything else.

13. Create a Budget NOW!

One of the things too many people do is trying to go through their financial lives without a plan or a budget. Bills come in, they pay them and hope that there will be enough at the end of the month to pay all the bills that come in. While that might have worked for us when we were in high school and possibly college, it really doesn't work for us well at all as we get older and life gets more complicated.

To be financially responsible, we need to know how much money comes in every month and how much money goes out in the form of our "standard" or essential bills and expenses. Only after we understand how much money we have and how much we spend can we manage our finances properly and effectively.

This is important because most of us will be saving for our retirement on a weekly or monthly basis. That is going to mean that we will be setting aside money every month out of our income. But even that might not be possible if we have no idea how much we can afford to put aside in the first place!

Saving for retirement is like saving for any other major expense.

It requires a plan that is achievable without too much sacrifice. If the sacrifice is too high, we will likely stop saving. But if we come up with a plan where we can accomplish our goals with little sacrifice, we stand a much better chance of keeping up the effort for the long-term.

Everyone should have a budget and that budget MUST be accurate and realistic. We must be honest with ourselves when it comes to what we spend and what we bring in. We might love to save $1,000 a month towards retirement but if we only have $1,000 left over after our essentials that would mean we would never be able to buy a dinner out, go to a movie, buy tires for the car or a new shirt!

How long do you think that might last? One month or possibly two??????

In that particular example we might figure on saving $500 and that might even be a stretch. But the main thing we are talking about is KNOWING what we spend not thinking about what we spend. It means tracking our income and expenses every month and setting aside money for all our expenses not just some of them.

Everyone should have a pretty thorough understanding of what comes in and what goes out every month. This is needed so when you are in the store and thinking about whether or not you should purchase something you will know how much money you have to work with every month. This will enable you to make informed and intelligent decisions and not decisions made out of guesswork.

But when it comes to retirement savings, we actually need two budgets! One budget for today and another budget for what we forecast our expenses are going to be once we retire. In most cases our retirement plan will also serve as our retirement budget.

It just makes sense to understand that we cannot come up with a figure of what we should have for our retirement if we have no idea what our retirement expenses are going to be! Yet many people do just that. They don't think about what their needs will be they just pick a figure out of thin air and think that should be enough!

It used to be that if you had a million dollars when you retired you could live like a king. But now a million just won't cut it unless you have a pension and other income on top of your savings! So you need to understand what you are going to need every year and then work from that to determine what needs to be saved.

If you are concentrating on your retirement then you want to know your current budget so you can figure out what the maximum amount of money you can save every month is going to be. Then you can use that figure to determine if you do save that much how much money you will have when you do retire. Then you can use your retirement budget to see if that will be enough money to see you through your retired years.

This is not guesswork. It requires planning and financial management. The great thing is that this is not rocket science and it is not difficult. Once you go through the initial process it is a simple thing to tweak it every year as your income and expenses change. Then it is a simple matter to compare where you are with where you should be and make any needed corrections.

The world is full of people who "thought" they had enough only to find out they are woefully short of money later on in their retirement. Don't become one of those people. Take the time and make the effort to come up with a budget for today to help fund your expenses of tomorrow. Then use a budget for tomorrow to make sure you will save enough.

14. Give the Gift of Retirement!

I am at an age right now where I don't really need all that much of anything when it comes to gifts. I have all the tools and clothes and gadgets and other things that I will ever need. Like most older people, if there is something we needed, we went out and bought it. So when birthdays and holidays come rolling around, we have to hunts and search for things to tell people to give us.

The same thing holds true for our spouses or partners as well. We go out and instead of getting each other what we need, we search all over for things just to have something for them to open or place under the Christmas tree. We spend a lot of money on things we would never buy for us in the first place.

If you are in that position, maybe you could agree with your spouse that instead of spending that $1,000 on gifts for each other this year you would take that money and put it in your retirement savings account.

If your kids want to give you something perhaps they might make a contribution as well. Or maybe they could pay some of your bills for you and you could take that money and put it towards retirement.

While I realize that this is a kind of a commercial or awkward approach to gift giving, it does accomplish a couple of things for all of us. It saves people a lot of time shopping for gifts most of us would never purchase for ourselves while at the same time gives us more space in our houses or apartments because it is not filled up with stuff we never wanted and will never use.

This idea might not appeal to a lot of people but it still is one way to fund retirement and make things easier on everyone else at the same time. If you find it is still awkward, then give each other gift cards that you can use for essential purchases and take the same amount of money as the gift cards and sock that away.

That would be a little less awkward while helping us accomplish pretty much the same thing.

15. Know Your Social Security

Most of us realize that we will get Social Security when we retire but a lot of us have very little idea just how much we are going to get. You cannot base your payments on what your parents got or what your neighbor gets because the actual amount is based on what you earned during your working career.

Another problem is the myth that Social Security is supposed to pay for our retirement. The fact is that Social Security was never meant to pay for your retirement. It was originally designed to help assist people in paying for their retirement expenses. In other words, people were still expected to save their own money and Social Security would assist them in covering the rest of their expenses.

The reason for this is that despite knowing that it is going to cost them money to live after they retire, people still refused to put anything aside for their later years.

So when it came time to retire, or when their companies forced them to retire, they had little money to pay for their expenses. So they either had to work at other jobs or go on public assistance. Social Security assured people of having some kind of income when they retired. Not enough to fully cover their expenses but a nice start.

Everyone should have some kind of idea what they will receive from Social Security when they get 5 -10 years from retirement. You can go to your local Social Security office or use on of the online calculators that are available to help you. Regardless of how you find out the amount, you should know it so you can plan better.

Social Security is based on the highest earning years in your work history. So if you can somehow increase your salary over the last 10-15 years of work then you will increase your benefit as well. That might mean changing jobs, getting a higher paid job, or just working as much overtime as you can to boost your salary and Social Security payments in the future.

Your financial advisor can talk to you about other options you might have when it comes to being able to increase your Social Security benefits. When couples are involved there are options as to who should collect on whose account and when you should file for benefits. It can get a little bit complicated but your advisor should be able to give you the information you need in order to plan properly and effectively.

16. Bank a Part Time Income

While we all hope to earn as much as we need to pay our current and future expenses, the reality of it is that sometimes things don't go quite the way we hoped or expected they would go. Sometimes we lose our jobs or our companies go out of business or the promotion we thought would happen went to someone else. Regardless of the reason sometimes we have to make alternative arrangements in order to bring some extra money into the household.

When it comes to saving for retirement, one option is to take a part time job to bring more money into the home so that you can save at a higher rate. Just a few extra hours and dollars a week can make a substantial difference when it comes to retirement savings.

If you think this is something that will be required or that this is something you would like to do, then it is best to start this earlier rather than later.

The longer you will have this money in your accounts earning interest and working for you the better it will be. For example working a part time job for two years at 40 or 50 will bring you more money at retirement than working two years at age 61.

In order to get the most benefit from your part-time income, if it is possible, have your entire check deposited directly into your retirement accounts. This way you will be less likely to take one check and spend it on a fancy dinner instead of investing it. If you are working a part-time job in order to do that sort of thing that is fine. But if you are working to fund your retirement, then do the direct deposit thing!

If you work at your part-time job long enough, it can also have the benefit of increasing your Social Security benefit when you retire because your earning would have been higher for those years. This will only hold true if the years you worked at your part-time job were among your highest earning years.

You should also be aware that sometimes working two jobs will result in either less of a tax refund or possibly evening resulting in your having to pay at the end of the year. This is because when you combine the two salaries it could place you in an overall higher tax bracket. But even if this is the case you would still have more money than if you had not earned the second income.

17. Start a Small Home Based Business

Another great way to save more money for your retirement is to start a small home based business using the skills, talents, knowledge and experience that you have gained over your life time. Though we all have the dreams of opening the next mega store or creating the next EBAY or Amazon that is not what we need to do in order to make a significant impact on our retirement savings.

A home-based business allows you to make an unlimited income while taking advantage of business tax deductions and other benefits. Your business might be a crafts business where you turn a hobby into a money making business. There is sometimes high demand for certain crafts products and you could do quite well.

Another benefit of a home-based business is that you do not have a set schedule, no rent or much overhead and you can work without a commute as well! The risk is low if you do it right and the costs to start a business like this are low as well.

Just keep is real and do not sink all your money into something that has little chance of success.

Almost any skill or talent can be turned into a home based business. If you have business experience you could offer your services as a consultant, open a resume writing service or do any number of other business related tasks or services. There are very few skills today that are not in demand by someone. Your only task is to find the best group to market your skills and then develop a cliental.

People who love to paint could sell their paintings. People who are handy around the house could do home repairs or handyman jobs for other people. There is always a demand for quality labor at reasonable prices! Even something as simple as offering to pick-up and delivery groceries or other services can bring in some extra money for you.

If this interests you, just make sure that you have all the licenses you might need in order to operate a legal business in your area. You do not want to get on the wrong side of the law! Start small and make sure there is a demand for the products and services you have to offer before investing a considerable amount of money.

Be careful of internet business opportunities because so many of them are scams and are just interested in taking your money and then running away. I would be very skeptical of any internet business opportunity. If all you have to invest is time you might want to give one a try but if they demand money to start or monthly fees, I'd try something else.

If you are making your own products though, the internet could be a great place to sell them. EBAY and other sites are great places to advertise your crafts. Online payment services like PayPal offer easy ways to process payments and ship your products to your customers. If you really think there could be a real market for your products and services, you can purchase a domain name and website for less than $15 and be up and running in now time!

Another benefit of starting a home based business is that these business can sometimes help bring in money after you retire as well. If you are doing something you enjoy why stop just because you retire? Continue your business, bring in more money and live better in retirement. There is not much of a downside in doing that!

Always remember that when you own a small business of any kind you need to report any income you make to the government and pay taxes on it. But the good side of that is that as a business you can get more tax deductions and also might be eligible for other retirement savings opportunities as well. Be sure to talk to your financial advisor about whether or not your home based business qualifies you for any special considerations or programs.

One word of caution when it comes to starting your own business. Small businesses are very customer service focused. They require a certain level of service and commitment in order to be successful.

If you are not the type of person who follows through on things then this is not for you. You would be better working for someone else part-time where they assume all the risk and commitment.

18. Health & Long Term Care Insurance

Though this might not be for everyone, medical insurance is something that must be part of everyone's retirement planning. Medical costs are among the highest and most volatile costs for retirees. Though Medicare will assume some of these expenses, it doesn't cover everything. Almost everyone will want to have some kind of additional coverage to help provide coverage and save some of their savings from medical costs.

Long-term care insurance helps protect you against the costs of having to stay in a nursing home for an extended period of time. With costs of those facilities going from $8,000-$20,000 a MONTH they can quickly burn through even the most impressive savings accounts!

Not everyone may qualify for long-term care insurance and the older you are when you apply the higher your premiums are going to be.

So if this kind of coverage appeals to you, then I would inquire about it now and not wait until you are close to retirement. The longer you wait the more expensive the yearly premiums are going to be and the more likely it might be that you develop a medical issue that would keep you from becoming approved.

Long-term care coverage is not inexpensive and there are several companies and whole load of options and policies that will make your head spin. My advice is to find an independent professional who can help guide you through the process and properly advise you. They can also file the forms for you and help you through the approval process.

As for other medical insurance, you should look into coverage that pertains to your specific needs. These coverages might include prescription drugs, physical therapy and other medical costs. Naturally the coverage levels come with their own costs and it is up to you to purchase what you think you will need and not necessarily more.

These types of insurance generally serve two purposes. First and foremost they help pay high bills for treatment that might be needed so your retirement savings will not be depleted as fast as it might have been. This is no small matter since non-insured medical fees can be staggering for most people.

The other part of this type of coverage is the peace of mind that it brings along with it.

With the right coverage we will not have to constantly worry about what we will happen when we or our partner should require advanced care or become a victim of a serious illness. During these times the last thing you need is to worry about losing all your money along with the medical concerns.

Unfortunately, these types of insurance, because they are targeted on the older people are also targets for scammers and people who are looking to make a quick buck at your expense. I would be wary of people who approach you for this type of insurance. If you are the one making the inquiry that is one thing. If you are being targeted, that is something else entirely.

Before signing any document do a thorough search on the company writing the policy and also the people who are representing them to you. If either of them are complaints or a lot of negative comments on the internet, be very careful. As I said, there are a lot of people who don't tell the truth or misrepresent things to unsuspecting people.

One area to be concerned with, especially when it comes to long-term care policies, are past rate increases. A few companies selling these types of policies have been known to raise rates as much as 20% a year! If the representative tells you that they cannot do that because they are regulated, don't get too comfortable with that either!

That is because when companies request rate increases they usually tell the state agencies that they can no longer afford to provide the insurance with this increase and they will have to pull out of the market if the request is not granted. Since the state does not want to have a lot of people without insurance, they will usually grant the increase. They might not admit it but just look at the track records.

When it comes to medical costs and insurance coverage, you need to factor these expenses into your retirement budget and you need to be overly generous because no one knows where these costs are going to be in the future. Medical costs over the last 10 years have been almost out of control and there is little indication that this is going to change in the near future.

We said it before and we will say it again. No one has ever complained that they had too much money to pay their expenses but the world is full of people who underestimated their needs and are paying for it now.

19. Retirement First, Kids Second

If you are a parent, you usually want to help your kid's out when it comes to education and other expenses that they incur right after they start out in life. But sometimes we need to step back and look out for our own future as well. That is because at this stage in time your children and you are in totally different situations.

You are either close to retirement or have 10 or fewer years before you think about retirement. While that might seem to be a long time for you, it really isn't when it comes to saving for retirement. Any commitments or actions you take at this stage in time could very well prove to be unrecoverable.

Your children, on the other hand, are just starting out in life and have 40 years or more before they have to worry about retirement. They have their own life ahead of them and they have plenty of time to make mistakes and recover from them. There is not much they cannot recover from at this point in time.

The most common expense that we think about when it comes to our children is college.

College today can cost $200,000 or more depending on where your child goes to school. Hopefully they will get some kind of scholarship to offset some of the cost but if they go away to school then you will have room and board to think about which can add another $15-20,000 a year just for that alone!

Our most common reaction is to take out a loan to help offset some of those expenses if we have not saved enough already. The problem with taking out such a loan at this stage in life is that is hampers our ability to save and exposes us to a huge financial risk should we be unable to repay those loans before we retire. Your child, however, will have over 40 years to repay their loans for their education.

This is an area where parents DEFINITELY need to see a financial advisor to determine the best way to fund a child's education. The child may have to take out student loans in their name and not in the parent's name. The parent can help them pay the loans off but they would be in the child's name.

It might even be that the parents tell the child they will have to pay for their education themselves or that the child pick a less expensive school closer to home so there are limited additional expenses. It might not be what the child wants to hear and it might not be what the parent wants to say but it is the reality in some households today.

One thing a parent must never do is deplete their retirement savings in order to pay for college.

Not only will there usually be huge penalties for withdrawing funds early, there will be very little time to replenish that money they was removed. Even if it could be replenished all the compound interest that would have been earned during those years would be gone.

The same would apply to helping children buy their first home or other expenses. Today we want to do so much for our children because everything costs so much more than it used to. But we need to also keep in mind that those same things that are more expensive for them now will also be more expensive for us later and we might not be able to afford them later if we help our children out now.

I am not advising any parent to abandon their children or not help them. What I am suggesting is that we look at such help from both directions and make decisions based on the risks to both sides and who is best to assume those risks. They can take out the loans in their name and you can help with repaying them to the best of your ability but the ultimate responsibility should be theirs.

Weddings are another expense that parents used to assume but that has also changed. With the cost of a wedding in some areas exceeding $40,000 this is something that many couples saving for retirement might not be able to safely afford.

If that is your situation you will need to sit down with your child and honestly tell them what you can afford, if anything at all. Though it might seem overly harsh to say, paying for a wedding or a college education is not a right for your children. These are things that parents should do because they WANT to and they CAN do not because their children expect them to do.

Another way of looking at these things is that if you jeopardize your retirement savings today and you run out of money later, it would be your children you would look to for help. You would not be happy about having to do that and they would not be happy about having to support you throughout your retirement.

The much better solutions is to be responsible now in your decisions and be open and honest with your children about what you can and cannot do to help them in their lives. It might be an awkward conversation to have now but it will be a lot less awkward than the one you might have to have later.

20. Save When Downsizing

As we go through life, our lifestyle changes. We go from being single to some of us becoming part of a couple. We go from a room in our parent's home to a small apartment to a small house and then to a larger one. We go from just the one or two of us to maybe 3, 4 or 5 or more of us. We get more possessions and more obligations and more expenses. Life gets more complicated and more expensive and, if we do everything right, our salaries and income adjust to our demands accordingly.

But then as we get older, the reverse starts to happen. The kid's leave to go out on their own, the larger house we used to need is now a bit too big and too labor intensive for us to keep up with. While we were buying food and clothes and paying utilities for 4 or 5 we are now buying the same things for just one or two.

In other words, life got more complicated and then started to get less complicated.

Because of this, our expenses later on in life are often lower than they were in earlier year even though things cost more now than they used to. All of this means that we now might have more available money every month than we were used to. While we might be tempted to take a well-deserved vacation and kick back and relax for a while, there is another alternative.

You can take advantage of these lower expenses to save more for our retirement.

For example, if we sell the larger house for $400,000 and purchase a smaller house or condo for $250,000 we can take that $150,000 left over and make a nice contribution to our retirement fund. We don't have to purchase a luxury car and a timeshare in Hawaii with that money!

On a lesser scale, if we were used to spending $500 a month on food and now spend $300, then why not take that extra $200 and direct deposit it every month into our retirement fund account? The same with the money we save now on clothes and other expenses.

If we were fortunate enough to be able to pay for our children's education and we finally paid that off, why not continue making those same payments to us instead? You have been used to paying them every month so continue to pay them in the future but pay them to you instead.

If you had been saving for your daughter's wedding every month and she just was married, keep making those payments as well but make them to your retirement fund. Life is so much about habits and once you have become used to something it is much easier to keep on doing it. Just redirect the focus from other things to you!

Downsizing can also help in making life easier. Do you really want all the work taking care of that big house when you are retired? Do you still intend on having the boat or the motorcycle in retirement as well? If not, why not start downsizing your assets as well and take the proceeds and deposit them into your retirement fund.

Think about that boat and motorcycle. Not only will you get the money from the sale but you no longer have to pay maintenance, registration costs and insurance on both of them. So not only do you get to save the money you sold them for but every year moving forward you can pocket the costs of the other things we just talked about! It's a win-win!

It is just a great thing when you realize that life not only gets less complicated in the later years but it also gets financially less demanding as well. As long as you take advantage of these changes as they take place you will find yourself in a much better and more financially secure place when you retire.

21. Catch up Savings

If you are above a certain age, you may be eligible to contribute more towards your retirement accounts every year. Commonly called the "catch-up" contribution, this allows people who might be slightly behind their goals to increase their savings during the last few years before they retire to create a better lifestyle for themselves.

Depending on which type of account you have, you might be able to contribute an extra $1,000 to over $5,000 every year. If you have a spouse they can do the same thing as long as their age qualifies them as well.

This catch up contribution will help you take better advantage of the pre-tax deduction and allow you to grow your retirement savings tax free even faster. Generally you have to be 50 or older in order to qualify.

Contact your plan administrator of your financial planner to find out how you can take best take advantage of the catch-up contribution to grow your savings.

22. Asset Protection & Estate Planning

One of the goals of every person entering the latter stages of life is how to best protect their assets from government and medical creditors. When we save protect we are not talking about "hiding assets" or doing anything illegal. What we are talking about is taking the steps necessary to safeguard what we have spent our entire life building for ourselves.

Though we are not asset protectors or lawyers, we do have some basic advice to at least get you thinking about what you should be doing in your situation. Here are a few things everyone should be checking into when it comes to safeguarding their assets:

If you don't have a will, get one prepared. If your estate is complicated or extremely large, a will can make it easier for your heirs to get what you intended them to get.

A will might even make it easier for your spouse to get what they deserve in case the children or others contest their inheritance. Wills are not expensive and you can even get a will kit to prepare one for yourself. But this is a one-time expense and you probably should get a lawyer or other qualified professional to create one for you. You will also need to pick an executor which is someone who will see that your instructions are carried out like you wanted.

Power of Attorneys and Medical Proxys are useful as well when it comes to making decisions for yourself and others in the future. These will allow you to speak for your spouse or other designated people in the case that they cannot make decisions for themselves or cannot communicate their wishes to others.

There are other documents such as life estates, revocable and irrevocable trusts and pother options for shielding assets from unexpected expenses or life events. But each of these options has its own befits and drawbacks so it is best to have a professional guide you so you can make the proper choice.

All of these things should be approached with one idea in mind. That is to protect your savings and assets so that you can live a happy and financially secure life until the end. Again, this is not about cheating the system or trying to avoid paying your fair share of taxes. But the bottom line is that the system doesn't really protect us as much as it should. So we need to take control of our assets and protect them to the best of our ability.

The two people that will play a major role in this will be a financial advisor to help you decide which assets require protection and a lawyer who specializes in asset protection and estate planning. There are so many things you can do to protect yourself you would be foolish not to pay the consultation fee and get some advice.

If you do decide to see a lawyer, make sure you choose one that specializes in estate planning and asset protection. This will give you the best chance of getting the most up to date advice.

One thing you should know is that there is often a waiting period from the time you move or transfer assets and when you can shield those assets from creditors and others. Sometimes it can be 5 years or more so it makes sense to start planning and making those decisions today.

Even though you might be healthy today you never know what might happen tomorrow or next month or next year. Remember the waiting period and the role it might play in your situation. You cannot get sick today, shield your assets tomorrow and go into a nursing home the next day and not have those assets count in your portfolio.

So really consider evaluating just how safe and protected your assets might be should you or your spouse or partner incur some serious medical or nursing home expenses.

This is not something to be taken lightly and you should at least have a consultation with a qualified professional to see if there are any weaknesses in your strategy.

Once again please understand that we are not estate planners or lawyers and you should not use the information in this chapter or any other part of this book as legal advice or as estate planning advice. These are just our observations meant to get you to think about looking into things and should not be considered as a specific plan of action. Everyone is different and everyone's situation is different so a lawyer or other professional is definitely the way to go.

23. Your Home

When it comes to your retirement savings. Many people do not factor the value of their home into their total assets. This can change your outlook on retirement considerably. On the opposite end of the spectrum, there are other people who do consider their home's value in their retirement and this can cause them problems as well. Let me explain.

For most of us, our homes are the most expensive or highly valued asset we have other than our retirement savings. The value of our home needs to be factored in to our retirement package because there are funds available should the home be sold. So if our home is worth $300,000, that represents about $300,000 more in cash that we will be able to have at our disposal during retirement.

Now that might seem like a powerful addition to our retirement and it really is. After all, over 30 years even without a penny of interest that $300,000 represents $10,000 a year or about $830 a month! That is a nice extra amount for most budgets.

But you must consider what will change when you sell that home. Once you sell the home you will have to find another place to live unless you will be living with family. So now you will have rent to pay which might be more expensive than what you were paying in monthly expenses with your home. So even though you have the "extra" $800 a month, that figure might be reduced by the extra rent you will need to pay.

On the positive side, selling your home and renting an apartment will stabilize your expenses because you will not have to worry about unforeseen repairs and damages. In addition, you will now have renters insurance instead of homeowners insurance and that will be less as well.

What we are trying to tell you is that you should factor in the value of your home when considering your retirement portfolio. But also keep in mind that a lot of things will change when you do sell your home and some of those will change your overall monthly expenses. These changes can be good or bad but you really need to understand them so you can plan accordingly.

Another aspect of selling your home might be selling your larger home and downsizing into a smaller one. We already discussed downsizing and selling a more expensive home and purchasing a smaller one, or selling a more expensive home and moving to another area where homes are less expensive should result in a cash windfall. But keep in mind that any time you move you incur moving expenses as well so those will take a bite out of your net profit.

Depending on your own situation, selling a home may result in taxes being paid on the profit you made on the home. Though sometimes there are exclusions or one time deductions you can take, depending on the sale price of the home you still might have to pay some taxes.

Because of this, I advise everyone that when you sell a home for a profit hire a professional to do your taxes for that year even if you usually do them yourself. I advise this because an experienced person will know what to deduct and how to report the sale properly. Even an innocent mistake can result in penalties and interest as well as the amount of tax due.

If you have a financial planner or advisor, consult them on the sale as well before you do sell the house. There might be advantages to selling at a particular time or other moves that should be made at the same time to lessen the taxes or increase your profits from the transactions.

So by all means factor in the cost of you home when you are determining what you will need for your retirement. But also be aware that you will still have to have somewhere to live and that means new or at least different expenses. So take those into consideration so you can forecast accurately.

24. No Premature Withdrawals!

Up to this point, we hopefully have saved a lot of money or at least now have a plan and the intention of saving more for our retirement. You can never have too much money for retirement. Even though you might think you have enough, you never really know. But now that you have it, we want you to keep it.

Throughout this book we have stressed one important concept. That is that you should save as much as you can while still being able to live a comfortable life. You should sacrifice but not to the point where you cannot day for essential expenses or the normal costs of living. If you try and save too much, eventually you will stop because there was too much sacrifice.

But there is another reason for not saving more than you can afford. That is the possible pressure or need to take money out of your retirement accounts to pay off debt that you incurred. We need to adopt a philosophy that once the money goes into a retirement account that it stays there.

We need to forget that it exists except for times when we evaluate our plan and make those changes we talked about.

There are several reasons for not withdrawing money from retirement accounts. Here are just a few:

First, there could be substantial penalties for early withdrawals. Sometimes a 10% penalty over and above the taxes you will have to pay on the amount you withdraw. So not only are you reducing the money you have I your account but you are paying a 10% fee and getting nothing whatsoever for it in return! This is like just throwing away 10% of your withdrawal!

Second, not only are you removing money from your account and reducing your savings, you are also losing the interest that the money would have earned every year until you retire. In many cases this will exceed the money you withdrew from the account! So that $5,000 withdrawal you made could wind up reducing your money at retirement by $10-15,000 after you figure in lost interest!

Third, once you make one withdrawal, it usually becomes easier to make additional withdrawals in the future. Once you see how your current financial needs can be so easily addressed without any sacrifice, the urge to use this approach in the future will become greater. The problem is that you are solving today's problems by mortgaging your future!

Some accounts allow you to make withdrawals in the form of a loan but even that has to be paid back and you would still lose the interest the funds would have earned had they been left in the account.

If you must make a withdrawal and there appears to be no other way for you to address your current needs, PLEASE talk to a retirement counsellor or financial advisor to see what they suggest you can do. Sometimes it might be a better idea to withdraw from one type of account than another or maybe they will find a better solution for you that does not involve touching your retirement savings.

Always keep in mind that you only have a certain amount of time to save for your retirement. Any time you remove funds from your account you are increasing the time you need to reach your goals. Though it might appear to be an easy fix for a current problem, removing funds now might cause you to delay your retirement or force you to save an even larger amount of money in the years ahead. If you remove too much money you may never be able to recover those funds in time for retirement.

The best way to keep from touching retirement funds is to keep living within your means and having other savings options with money in them to meet current and unexpected expenses. Though this approach might not cover every unforeseen expense, it will keep you and your retirement accounts safe from withdrawals for most of the years ahead.

Though credit and loans are never a really great idea because of the interest involved, getting something like a home equity line of credit where you only pay interest when you need the money might be a better safeguard. There are no penalty or other fees other than the cost of opening the line of credit and those costs are quite low if your credit rating is good.

With all types of credit, however, they only work when you use them responsibly and do not abuse them. Check with your financial advisor or counsellor to determine which is the best course of action for you and your spouse.

25. Plan Last Minute Major Purchases

When it comes to how much money we will need going into retirement, you have to take into consideration two things. How much you will save and how much you will spend. It figures that if you spend less in retirement you will have to save less in order to reach your objectives. That is why people who want to retire and live on Maui will need more money that those who will live in the back woods of Kentucky. That is not to say that one area is nicer to retire in than the other. It just means real estate and other costs are likely to be different.

Since we have spent the vast majority of this book covering different ways of saving more and having more for retirement, let's switch gears a bit and talk about things you can do from the expense side to allow your savings to go further and last longer.

First, I always recommend doing a financial audit on your expenses every other year or so in order to identify potential areas of savings. Things change over the years and there might be better alternatives for those expenses you do have now that will help you save money.

For example, switching cable or satellite providers might help you take advantage of some bundled services and save possibly $100 a month. You should re-evaluate insurance coverages and possibly even the need for continuing certain insurance at all. Over the years our needs change and our coverage should change with them. Sometimes this results in savings and sometimes we find we are underinsured. Either way it is smart to know what you are paying and be sure you are getting the best deal possible.

You should also decide if you are still paying for stuff you don't use anymore. Are you still paying for cable channels you don't watch because at one time the kids wanted or needed them? Are you paying for services you don't use anymore but never cancelled? Take every bill and verify you still need that product or service. If you do, then keep it or look for a better deal. If you don't need it, cancel it.

If you can save just $100 a month by reducing expenses that amounts to $1,200 a year and over 25 years you would save $30,000! All while keeping your standard of living pretty much the same! You just can't beat that!

But one very cool way to dramatically change you retirement expenses is by taking care of large expenses that you know are coming before you retire and while you are still working.

Remember that while you are working you always have a greater ability to handle larger purchases and make changes to accommodate unexpected expenses.

Start by thinking about what major expenses are likely going to be needed close to retirement. Do this around 5 years before you retire. This will give you time to address those expenses on your terms and on your schedule which almost always results in you paying less for most everything.

For example, if your car has 90,000 miles on it and you are 3 years away from retirement, try and save some money and buy a replacement vehicle, either new or late model used, before you retire. That way you will not have to incur a $20,000 or more cash expense while you are on a fixed income. After all, you will need a car and you know your current model is close to the end of where it is economical to drive and repair. Don't pay full price but continually search for the best possible deal. You can drive the old one until the perfect new one comes along and not be forced to purchase one out of desperation.

The same goes for other expenses as well. If you plan on staying in your home for a while, think about what is going to need work or replacement. If your driveway is falling apart, get it replaced while you are still working and on your timetable. You can shop around to get the best deal and pay for it with your salary not your savings.

Is your furnace or heating system and central air conditioner in good shape? If it is 20 years old then maybe you might want to consider replacing it now with an energy efficient model that will not only last you many more years but cost you less in electricity to operate.

A high efficiency gas or oil unit will cost you less in heating bills as well. Plus, you pay that expense off while you are still earning your full salary.

The list can go on and on. If your refrigerator is 20 years old or if your roof is worn or has been giving you problems, consider acting on those things as well. Your goal should be to have as many of the possible major expenses addressed and taken care of by the time you retire. This will enable you to have more of your retirement money to actually live on with less going towards major repairs and other expenses.

Now there is also another approach to this that might be better for those of you who either are not sure about an expense or who are not sure whether they will be living in the same home 5 or 10 years from now. In those cases, it might not be cost effective to put major money into a home that you might soon sell. Though new appliances and a new roof will add to the resale value, the added value might not come close to the costs involved.

Other potential items such as the air conditioner or even the automobile might last another 10 years. With these you never know. Some people dislike replacing things proactively and they feel that is like throwing money away. If you are one of those people, why not think about taking a different approach?

Instead of actually purchasing those things, open a savings account and place the money for those expenses in your account so when they do really break or are needed, you have the money for them. If the money is used to fund those expenses that's what it is there for. If it isn't needed, you can always use it for something else. A little nest egg is always nice to have around.

We already mentioned that no one really knows how long that roof or air conditioner is really going to last? If it lasts 10 years, then maybe you get away with not replacing it or replacing it just once over the course of your retirement and not twice. It's taking a risk while still saving some money for those kind of expenses should they pop up.

One potential downside is that waiting to take care of something might result in paying a higher price for those repairs or purchases. Putting off buying that replacement vehicle might cost you another few thousand because of price increases. Labor charges almost never go down and usually rise so you might pay more for repairs and other work if you do them later instead of now.

You should have a list of potential things that you feel you are going to have to purchase or address over the next 10 years and then decide which are best to handle now and which should be held off until later or when they are actually needed. Chances are there will be a few items that fit in either of these categories. Having the list will enable you to more accurately forecast future needs as well as set a schedule of addressing some or most of them by the time you are ready to retire.

The whole idea is to reduce the overall burden on your finances by taking care of as much as possible while you are still working. There will be things that you just know need to be done and you should take care of those on your schedule so you can enter retirement with a clear head and the knowledge that you did the best you could to prepare yourself both from the savings side and the expense side.

26. Postponing Retirement

In a perfect world, we would all retire when we were ready to retire. For some of us that do not particularly like our jobs, or when out work is physically demanding, that might be when we are 50 or 55 while others who truly love their jobs might prefer to work until they are 70 or 75! There is no perfect choice other than what feels right for us as individuals.

When we have enough money to properly fund our retirement with plenty to spare or tide us over even when the cost of living goes higher and interest rates go lower, the decision when to retire is ours alone. But when we don't have enough money, or when we are calling things a little bit too closely for comfort, we might wish to consider putting off retirement for a year or two or even longer.

There are many reasons and incentives for doing this. Here are just a few:

First, working longer gives you longer to save the money you will need for retirement. That means you can save more money to help you live better and more comfortable during your retirement. If you can save $15,000 a year and you worked an extra 2-4 years, that would add $30-60,000 into your retirement fund. That might make a big difference when it comes to how you live moving forward.

Second, with everything else being equal, every year you work longer is one less year you will have to fund your retirement. So if you are going to live until 95 and you retire at 55, then you will have to fund 40 years of retirement. But if you worked until you were 70, then your retirement fund would only have to cover 25 years! So you would have more money per year because you worked longer.

Third, every year past your Social Security retirement age that you put off applying for benefits will result in an increase in your monthly benefit. So the longer you work, the larger your Social Security monthly check will be. So in addition to being able to save more money, you will be earning more money every month from Social Security. If you have any pensions or other types of retirement programs that pay a monthly benefit those might increase as well. You will have to check with the plan's administrator to see if this applies to your particular plan or benefit.

Fourth, every year you work you will be bringing in your full salary which may enable you to not only save more for retirement but also pay off outstanding debt or prepare yourself for retirement. The better financial shape you are in entering retirement the better off you will be and the longer your retirement savings will last.

For you there may be more advantages as well as a few disadvantages.

If you are in good health and have a reasonable expectation of a long and healthy retirement, it might make sense for you to work a little bit longer to enable yourself to live a happier and more secure retirement. But if you are in poor health and are not a good candidate for a longer retirement, that might make you rethink the working longer option because you might not live long enough to go through your savings anyway. It sounds morbid but it is something to think about.

But keep it real when you make this call. Having terminal cancer is one thing but a severe cough does not necessarily indicate you won't have a full recovery and live until 95! Remember the choices you make today you will have to live with tomorrow!

If you truly love your job and it is one of the few pleasure in your life, sticking with it for a few more years as long as you are healthy enough to stand the stress and exertion that goes along with it should be fine. But if you don't enjoy your work, or if it is too stressful or physically demanding, working longer might not be a good option for you unless you can change jobs to something more to your liking. Again, this decision is up to you.

Whatever you may decide, just make sure it is the right decision for you. It might not be the easiest decision or the right choice might not be the most pleasant or enjoyable choice but you do have the future to consider. Very often once we make the choice we cannot simply decide in a year or two to go back to work at the same job at the same salary. So give it some thought now and make the right decision now so you can live the best life later on.

Wait!
That Was 26 Ways
To Save for Your
Retirement!
But We Have More
To Tell You!

How About Some
Bonus Content!

Just Turn the Page
For More Great Information!

27. Supplementing Retirement

Despite our best efforts, sometimes life throws us a few curveballs that make life and saving money more difficult than we thought it was going to be. We have to sometimes deal with employment issues, medical issue, unexpected expenses that will throw any budget into chaos and a host of other things. When those happen there is nothing we can do except pick ourselves up, dust ourselves off and try to get back to as close to normal as we can.

If we find ourselves short of our retirement savings goals, then we might have to extend our working years or think about ways to supplement our retirement with a second income of some type. Then we use that money to reduce the amount of money we will have to take out of our savings every year thereby making it last longer.

Some options might be to make money by selling things you make from a hobby or other skills or talents. You might decide to pick up a part-time job to both keep you busy and help with the expenses.

For those of you who just need a little extra over the course of the year you might be able to find seasonal employment where you only have to work a month or two out of the year and still bring money in to help out a bit. Everyone is different and everyone's situation is different. But if you still are feeling well but are a little short on your retirement savings, then a part-time job might be just what the doctor ordered.

Some people might even make an arrangement with their current employer that they are going to retire but will still come in the office one or two days a week just to keep active. This will allow them to earn some extra money while the employer still has access to many years of experience that is still in your head.

You might even be able to eliminate the bad parts of your old job to make your part-time job even better. For example maybe you loved the job but hated the travelling. So you see if you can come back part-time, and do the rest of your job without doing any of the travelling. This might be something your employer would agree to.

Working just one or two days a week would still give you 5 days off a week which is more than enough to take small trips and outings whenever you wanted to while still keeping your mind active and some money coming through the bank account. Another benefit to this arrangement is that it will almost always pay you a higher wage per hour than other part-time employment.

28. After Retirement

Ok, this is the last chapter of the book so it makes sense to talk about the last chapter of life and retirement as well. Though it might seem a bit morbid, we all need to embrace the fact that at some point, we will cease to roam this great earth of ours. No matter how much money we have or how much we are loved and respected, no one lives forever. The only thing we can do is live well and eat healthy and try to prolong our lives.

Unfortunately, even dying costs money these days and funerals are not inexpensive. Most people plan to set aside some money I their retirement for final expenses so they are not a burden to their children or to the surviving spouse or partner. Exactly how much this should be depends on where you live and what kind of funeral arrangement you want to make.

If it is just you then whatever you want you should have as long as you have the money to pay for it. If there is a surviving spouse involved then you should make sure that your arrangement will not cause your partner undue financial hardship after you are gone.

I am just saying all of this because final expenses need to be a part of your retirement plan. The process is not pleasant but you should give some thought to what you want or expect upon your passing and save enough money to fulfill those expectations.

So decide what you want, put it in writing and share it with your children so there is no disagreement or confusion as to what you want and then do your best to fund it. Most people want to do this so they do not become a burden on their children or other loved ones. Hopefully you feel that way as well.

Conclusion

If we plan things right, retirement can be a wonderful time where we get the chance to do more of what we love in life and less of what we don't like. There is no more work related stress or the monotony of doing the same job day in and day out. We get to spend more of our time like we want to spend it than ever before.

When you stop and think about it, we really need and deserve this time for ourselves after spending our lives taking care of family and loved ones. So now retirement makes this our time. It is our time to sit back and watch others take care of the rat race and the rest of the world. It's a really cool time for most people.

But we need to realize that even though retirement for some of use might be several decades away, it is what we do now that will help determine how well we live later in life. We can choose to live every day like it's our last and spend every penny as we make it or we can look into the future and prepare ourselves now for what lies ahead.

The choice is ours.

The one universal truth when it comes to retirement is that we must not, or even cannot, sit back and expect other people or the government to pay our way through retirement. It just doesn't work that way. Sure government will help us and will provide money and programs to assist us during retirement but the ultimate responsibility for our retirement lies with us.

Not with the government or our employer but with us. We must take responsibility for both our present and future.

Today there seems to be more and more people with entitlement issues in the world. They feel the world and government somehow owe them something for what they did during their life. Well, the reality is that if you want a nice retirement, there are people and programs that will assist you but you also have to do your part as well.

Our part starts with savings.

As we all tend to live longer these days, the cost of retiring has gone steadily upwards. In other words, we need more money now than ever before and that means saving more and for longer period of time than ever before. We must start early and we must save our money. If you don't then we are going to have to rely on hitting the lottery and the odds on that happening are not that good at all.

With all of this, I would like to issue everyone reading this book a challenge.

I would like each person reading this book to go and get a pad and pencil and write down at least 3 ways that you are going to start saving for retirement. Then go out and start doing those 3 things and start investing that money into your future.

Come up with a real and accurate plan and forecast for what you are going to need and then write down some specific action steps you are going to take to help turn that retirement plan into your reality. Don't put this off. Do it now. Start simple but just start!

You can, and should, go back and modify your plan as your life changes. But always make sure that you are headed in the right direction. Though it might seem overly harsh, there is only one or two people you can really count on in life when it comes to achieving your goals. One of those people is you and the other is your partner. Even some times you cannot count on your partner either and it is just you.

Accept any help that comes you way but do not wait for it to arrive because it might never show up. Instead, take the bull by the horns and do what needs to be done to get you where you want to be. You will be glad you did and you will be glad you started early.

Early on in this book we said that no one ever complained about having too much money in retirement. But we also said the world is full of people who regret not taking the right action earlier in life. As this time you need to decide which one of those people you are going to become.

Are you going to be the one trying to figure out how to spend your money in retirement or are you going to be the one who has all the regrets? As with most things in life the choice is going to be yours.

Make the right choice..............

Retirement Resources

Interest Calculators

http://calculators.bankrate.com

http://www.interest.com/calculator/

Social Security Administration

http://www.ssa.gov

Application for Benefits Quote

http://socialsecurity.gov/retirement/retirement.htm

Credit Rating & Credit Scores

http://www.creditkarma.com

The above listed sites are for education and informational purposes only. We are not affiliated with these sites nor do we have any connection with them. Therefore we are not responsible for any or all of the information contained on these sites. Nor are we responsible for the accuracy of any calculations or the decisions resulting from those calculations. The reader accepts total responsibility for the use of any or all of these sites.

For More Information and some other great titles to help you get more out of retirement and life in general, please visit our website at:

http://www.26ways.com

When you visit be sure to sign up for our mailing list for free books, information and other great benefits! Remember,

IT'S FREE!

www.ingramcontent.com/pod-product-compliance
Lightning Source LLC
Chambersburg PA
CBHW071800200526
45167CB00017B/714